Learn Hypnosis... *Live!*

Updated Third Edition

Accelerated Hypnotherapy Certification Training

(714) 408-4281 · (800) 497-6614
www.transformdestiny.com

Learn Hypnosis... *Live!* Workbook
Live Certification Training

Published by Transform Destiny, www.transformdestiny.com

ISBN: 1946607002
ISBN-13: 978-1-9466070-0-3

Printed in the United States of America
10 9 8 7 6 5 4 3 2

Table of Contents

Welcome!

Welcome to our Hypnotherapy Certification Course. As you progress through this program, you will acquire a skill that will remain with you for the rest of your life. This class is based upon unique methods that have been developed from more than 30 years of experience in hypnotherapy and taught to more than 100,000 students around the world.

Hypnosis is as old as civilization itself and has been practiced under many names since time immemorial. However, it was not until 1958, when it was officially recognized by the American Medical Association, that Hypnotherapy began to come into its own. Since then, great strides have been made, but we know that they are nothing compared to achievements that will come in the future as new and exciting uses of Hypnotherapy come to light.

These classes are designed to be a hands-on learning experience. I encourage you to ask questions if you do not understand the material presented. Please ask for my help if you have difficulty with any of the techniques demonstrated in class. My goal is to provide a safe environment in which you are allowed to make mistakes and feel comfortable knowing that there is a trained professional nearby to assist you. With my help you will develop the skills you need.

After completing this course, you will be qualified to be a professional Hypnotherapist and may immediately begin practicing as such.

However, additional education, culminating in becoming a more advanced Hypnotherapist as well as an NLP Practitioner, TIME Techniques™ Practitioner, EFT Practitioner and Success/Life Coach, is available if you are interested in adding to your skill set and earning more professionally.

Now please, sit back, relax, and enjoy the course!

About Transform Destiny's Founder

Michael Stevenson MNLP, MTT, MHt is a professional hypnotherapist, coach and trainer and a Master Trainer of Hypnotherapy, Neuro-Linguistic Programming (NLP), TIME Techniques™, Emotional Freedom Techniques and Coaching. He's had specialized training in Advanced Parts Therapy, and is a certified Master Success Coach and coaches in the fields of Business and Personal Development.

Michael is a best-selling author and an international speaker. He has hypnotized tens of thousands of people around the world through his products and in person and is considered one of the world's foremost experts on the subjects of hypnosis and NLP. Michael is a dynamic presenter on a wide variety of topics ranging from personal growth to sales training.

Formerly in the IT field, Michael became interested in hypnosis when he used it to quit a years-long smoking habit. Realizing the power of hypnosis, Michael searched high and low for every available book on the subject. Realizing that books alone could not give him all the tools, he began to seek out and to attend the exact course you're attending this weekend, eventually achieving the honorable title of Master Trainer and purchasing the rights to the course.

Between speaking engagements, Michael and his wife and business-partner Kayla travel the world full time while serving tens of thousands of people through their companies, Transform Destiny and Influence to Profit.

You can email Transform Destiny for help, support and to enroll in other courses at cs@transformdestiny.com or by calling 800-497-6614 toll-free in North America or 714-408-4281 direct.

Michael has hand-picked your trainer for this weekend based on their expertise in the field and their ability to teach and train the material. You are in the best hands possible and we all hope you enjoy this weekend as the life-changing event we know it will be for you.

-Michael, Kayla and the Entire Transform Destiny Team

Notes

For Your Future Development

Future Trainings and Programs from Transform Destiny and Influence to Profit:

Business Track

The Inner Circle Coaching and Mastermind Program

Professional one-on-one coaching, mentoring, masterminds and business consulting with Transform Destiny and Influence to Profit founder, Michael Stevenson

Speaking to Profit
6 Days

Speak and sell from stage with charisma and character

Publishing to Profit
3 Days

Write, Edit, Publish and Market your Book

Marketing to Profit
4 Days

Modern, proven marketing strategies to create more profit and freedom

Influence to Profit
4 Days

Ethically influence and persuade people everywhere you go

The Irresistible Elevator Pitch Formula, NLP Copywriting Mastery, or other introductory courses

Learn business skills rooted in NLP

Certification Track

The *Accelerate* NLP Coaching and Mastermind Program

Professional one-on-one education, coaching, mentoring, masterminds, and business consulting to become a successful Hypnotherapist, Coach, NLP Practitioner, Master Practitioner, and/or Trainer

Master Trainer Development Program

TIME Master Trainer, Hypnotherapy Master Trainer Included, EFT Master Trainer Included, Coach Master Trainer Included

Training Materials Included: PowerPoints, handouts, manuals, logistics manuals, etc.

Trainer's Training & Evaluation

18 Days – Master Practitioner Required
TIME Trainer Included
Hypnosis Trainer Included
Coach Trainer and EFT Trainer Included

Master Practitioner Training

15 Days -- Practitioner Prerequisite
Master **TIME** Techniques Included
Master Hypnotherapist Included
Master Coach Included

NLP Practitioner Training

7 Days -- No Prerequisite
TIME Techniques, Hypnotherapist, EFT and Coaching Included

Create Your Life, Learn Hypnosis... Live! CORE Success and Life Coach Training or other introductory courses

16 - 20 Hour Courses, No Prerequisites

Notes

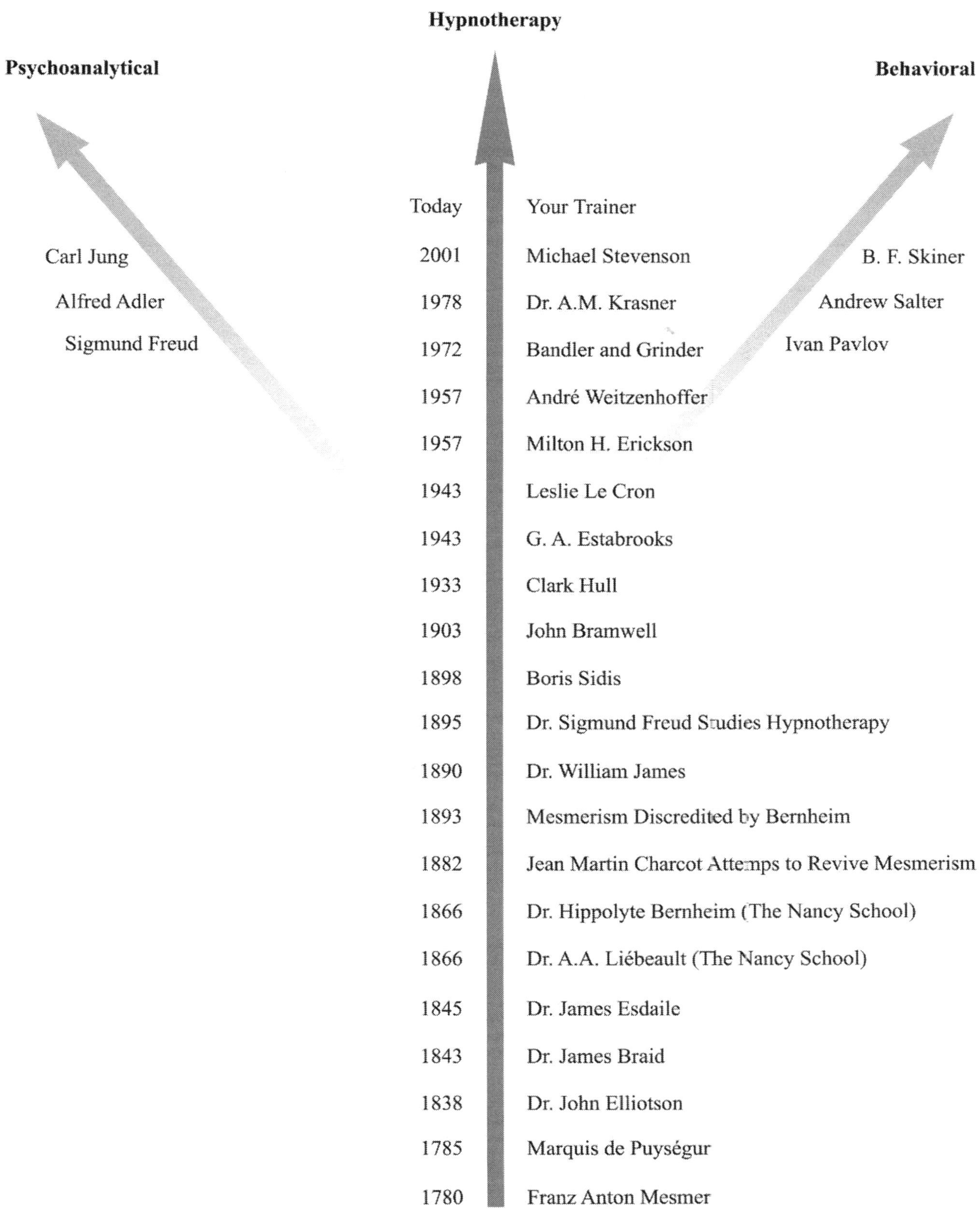

Hypnotherapy

Psychoanalytical

Carl Jung

Alfred Adler

Sigmund Freud

Behavioral

B. F. Skiner

Andrew Salter

Ivan Pavlov

Today	Your Trainer
2001	Michael Stevenson
1978	Dr. A.M. Krasner
1972	Bandler and Grinder
1957	André Weitzenhoffer
1957	Milton H. Erickson
1943	Leslie Le Cron
1943	G. A. Estabrooks
1933	Clark Hull
1903	John Bramwell
1898	Boris Sidis
1895	Dr. Sigmund Freud Studies Hypnotherapy
1890	Dr. William James
1893	Mesmerism Discredited by Bernheim
1882	Jean Martin Charcot Attemps to Revive Mesmerism
1866	Dr. Hippolyte Bernheim (The Nancy School)
1866	Dr. A.A. Liébeault (The Nancy School)
1845	Dr. James Esdaile
1843	Dr. James Braid
1838	Dr. John Elliotson
1785	Marquis de Puységur
1780	Franz Anton Mesmer

Notes

Prime Directives of the Unconscious Mind

1. Preserves the Body

2. Is A Servant, Likes to Follow Orders

3. Is Highly Moral

4. Stores All Memories

5. Thinks and Communicates in Symbols

6. Does Not Process Negatives

Notes

How the Mind Interprets

Loveisnowhere

Theytoldhimtobeatthefrontdoor

They are visiting relatives

Would you rather have an elephant eat you or a gorilla?

How many times does the letter "F" appear in the sentence in the box?
(include both upper and lower case)

Finished files are the result of years of scientific study combined with the experience of many years of experts.

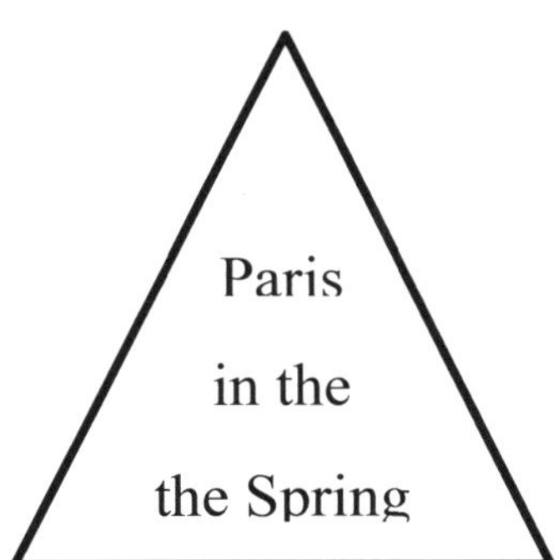

The sentence below is printed backwards. Read the sentence once from right to left.

".rat eht saw tac ehT"

Notes

What is Hypnosis?

Hypnosis Is Not...	Hypnosis Is...
Sleep	An Awake and Aware State
A State of Unconsciousness	Rapport With Your Unconscious
Being Gullible	Imagination
Being Weak-Minded	Exercise for Your Mind
A Loss of Self-Control	The Ultimate Display of Self-Control

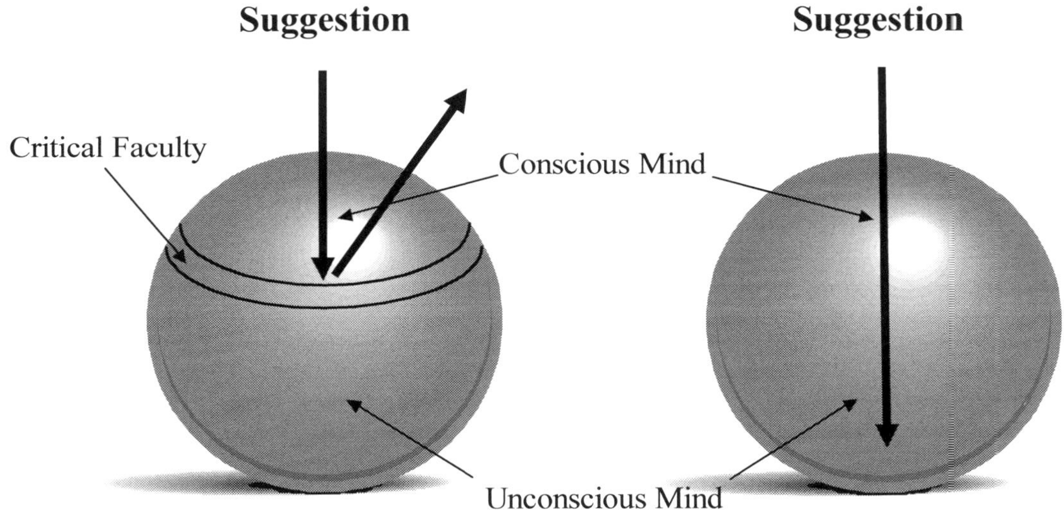

"Your clients will be your clients because they are out of rapport with their unconscious minds."

- Milton Erickson

Notes

The Krasner Method of Hypnotherapy

1. Demystify Hypnosis (What Hypnosis Is Not)

2. Explain Hypnosis (What Hypnosis Is)

3. Interview

4. Suggestibility Tests

5. Induction

6. Convincers

7. Change Work

8. Bring Them Up

Notes

Step 1 - Demystify Hypnosis

What Hypnosis is Not

"Let me tell you about hypnosis. You will not feel hypnotized, nor will you be out of control. You've seen hypnosis shows, haven't you…"

"You will hear everything…"

Demo

"Let me demonstrate to you what hypnosis really feels like, Close your eyes please (pause 5 seconds). That's it, it feels just like that!"

"You will be in total control…"

Demo

"Let me show you what I mean. Close your eyes, put your feet together place your hands in your lap, now go into the corner please and stand on your head…BY THE POWER OF HYPNOSIS bark like a chicken!"

Remember – You want them to know that there will be no "weird" feeling, no loss of consciousness or hearing. And they need to know that they are responsible for their own motivation and participation.

Notes

Step 2 - Explain Hypnosis

What Hypnosis Is

"The body is only a robot, controlled by the mind. What the mind sees, the body tends to do."

Demo

"… Let me give you an example…"

Remember – Once the misconceptions are handled, it is important to get into the "body is a robot" theory. The lemon demonstration is excellent for this.

Hypnosis works so well because it creates thoughts so realistic, the body reacts biochemically.

Notes

Step 3 - Interview

"… How **will** your life improve **when** you __________…"

(Do this process three times)

3 Keys to a Successful Interview:

1. Stated in the positive

If the client says a negative, then you respond:
"If you aren't _________, what are you?"
"If you don't _________, what will you do?"

2. Behavioral

If the client says a state/emotion, then you respond:
"When you have __________, what will you be doing?"
"When you are __________, what will you be doing?"

3. Specific

How to get more specific…
"Who, what, where, when, how specifically?

Remember – The more detail you receive during the interview the better, because you will be taking the information you receive and applying it to step 7, the therapy. An incomplete interview will result in an incomplete therapy, while a detailed, accurate interview will result in a detailed accurate therapy. Listen very carefully to the client's answers. They will give you the words to use in his therapy session. They are telling you what is important to him, and what his motivation is. Write down what they say.

Notes

Step 4 - Suggestibility Tests

(Never call them "tests" in front of the client the client)

"Let's do some fun experiments for your unconscious mind…"

Sway Test

Book & Balloon Test

Finger Vise Test

Notes

Step 5 – Induction

Three Keys to Successful Induction:

1. Vocal Timbre (Raspiness of the voice)

2. Vocal Tone

3. Tempo/Speed

Remember – ***What*** **you say is not nearly important as** ***how*** **you say it. Keep these three keys in mind when assisting your client into hypnosis.**

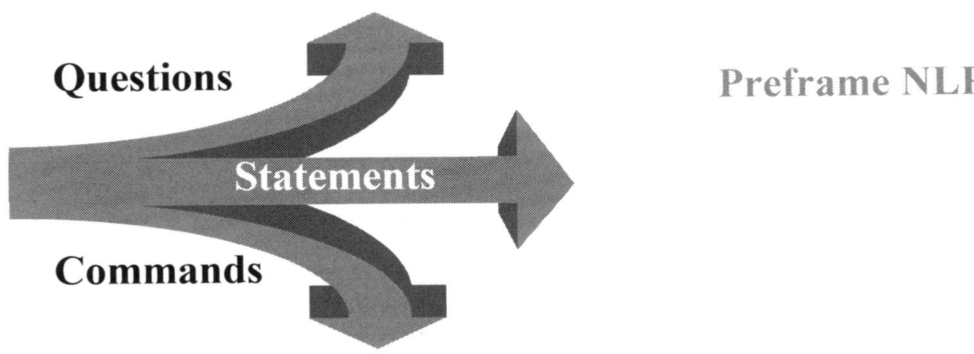

Notes

Sample Induction – Follow the Script

Sit back, relax, and just close your eyes. In a very few moments, you're going to be more relaxed than you've ever known yourself to be.. I'm going to mention certain parts of your body, and as I do, I want you to just feel that part begin to relax -- just feel that part just begin to relax. In order to help you relax, I want you to imagine yourself in a wonderfully magical forest. It's almost night time, and the sky is a beautiful indigo blue, the stars are coming out and the moon is lighting up the rich forest trees. Off in the distance, you hear the hypnotic sounds of a bubbling brook, and the crickets seem to be lulling you to sleep. And as you lie motionless, you begin noticing a wonderfully white light just above your head.

This white light is the most relaxing light you could imagine, and as it begins to lower around the crown of your head, you seem to be touched with a desire and willingness to relax deeper and deeper, with every breath you take. Continuing to lower now, it begins to touch the forehead, and as it does, I want you to feel all the little frown lines, all the little worry lines in the forehead, just seem to disappear. The forehead smoothes out, feels so relaxed, and you feel this relaxing light coming around the eyes. Now the eyelids seem to become very, very heavy, so heavy they don't even seem to want to open. They may flutter a little bit, but that's OK, just feel how heavy they are - and as the relaxation comes down around the facial muscles now, all the little muscles in the facial area just begin to relax.

Relaxation comes further down around the mouth now, and all the hundreds of little muscles around the mouth just start to relax... so much so, that the lower jawbone becomes heavy, and the teeth part. The mouth may even open up a little bit with relaxation as you continue deeper and deeper relaxed. Feel this relaxation now around the lower jawbone, and behind the ears so that all the little nerve endings behind the ears just seem to relax as you continue deeper and deeper, and even deeper. The relaxation goes to the back of the neck now, down around the shoulders, so much tension seems to go to our shoulders, but now you feel the shoulders just begin to relax. You can even feel them drop a little. The relaxation seems to go to the backbone now, and as it goes down the spinal column, it seems to go out to the sides, so that every muscle, every nerve, and every fiber in the back just seems to relax.

The relaxation seems to come now to the small of the back, and around the bottom. This warm sense of relaxation comes to the back of the thigh now, and into the hollow of the knee, around the calf of the leg, around the heel, to the bottom of the foot, and each and every toe just relaxes even more, and more, as you go deeper, deeper, and even deeper. Calm, very peaceful, very relaxed. And now, if necessary, allow yourself to shift your body however you need to in order to become even more comfortable, and become even more and more relaxed.

Notes

We are going to proceed to relax the rest of you now. Starting with the throat muscles, feel the throat muscles just start to relax. The relaxation comes down the fronts of the shoulders, down the upper arm, over the elbow, down the forearm, to the hand, and each and every finger just relaxes more, and more and more, as you go deeper, deeper and deeper relaxed. Just relaxing , doing so very, very well now, as you continue to relax.. Feel the relaxation now coming back to the throat muscles, down into the chest, and all the muscles and organs within the chest now, just begin to relax. This relaxation continues down to the stomach area, and all the muscles and organs within the stomach just seem to relax. This warm sensation of relaxation goes down into the thighs, over the knees, down the shinbone, across the instep of the foot, and into the foot itself, and each and every toe just relaxes more, and more, as you go deeper and deeper, relax deeper, and you continue deeper, and even deeper calm, very, very relaxed.

Now I want you to imagine yourself standing in this forest, and at the base of the feet is a beautiful stone stairway that leads downward into a very safe, valley of relaxation. This staircase will lead you into a profound state of deep, deep hypnosis. We're going to go down these stairs now, and as I count backwards from ten to zero each number will take you even deeper, and deeper, and even deeper. When you are ready to go down these stairs, simply nod your head please... (pause) that's right, very good.

Ten. Take that first step down. Nine, deeper, deeper. Eight, way down now. Seven, deeper, deeper. Six deeper, feeling very relaxed. Five, deeper, deeper. Four, you are going into a deep state of hypnosis now. Three, going deeper. Two, relaxed to even move, feeling very calm. One.

At the next number you will enter this beautiful place of peace and tranquility called deep, deep hypnosis. More relaxed and peaceful than you've ever known yourself to be. Is that OK with you? Nod your head please. (pause) Wonderful, Zerooooo.

Notes

Step 6 - Convincers

Heavy Eyes

"I'm going to count from one to three. With each number I count, your eyelids will become heavier and heavier. At the count of three you'll find that you can't open your eyes, even if you try. You'll find with a little bit of delight, you simply cannot open them. One, two, three."

Important: Cancel the suggestion: "…That's fine, don't even try anymore, they're just too heavy… the eyelids are returning to normal now"

Heavy Arm

"In a moment I'm going to count from one to five. With each number I count, your right arm will get heavier and heavier. So heavy, In fact, that when you try to lift it won't go up… just too heavy… 1, 2, 3, 4, 5. Concentrate on your right arm… notice how heavy it is… so very heavy. Go ahead and try, and find out with a little bit of delight, that it just won't lift. It's just too heavy.

Important: Cancel the suggestion: "…That's okay, it's too much work, it's just too heavy the arm is returning to normal now"

Light Arm

"And now I want you to imagine that there is a string tied around your left wrist and attached to the other end of that string is a large, bright-red, beautiful helium balloon, floating up, up, to the sky. As I count from one to three, your left arm will lift and go higher with that beautiful balloon. One, two, three."

Important: Cancel the suggestion: When <u>you're ready to make this change</u>, just allow the arm to drop back down to your lap, sending you ten times deeper than you are, even now. That's right…

Convincers serve THREE major purposes:

1. ______________________________

2. ______________________________

3. ______________________________

Notes

Step 7 – Change Work

Direct Suggestions - *Authoritative commands and/or post hypnotic suggestions*

End Result Imagery - *The answers from step #3—The Interview*

Remember – The more information you receive from the step #3, the interview (*How will your life improve when you…*), the more detailed your therapy will be.

Advanced: Metaphors - *Symbolic stories that parallel the client's outcome*

Notes

The Art of Suggestion: Layers of the Mind

Suggestions can occur on many levels. The most powerful influence occurs when all levels are aligned.

Notes

The Art of Suggestion: Targeting Layers

Results

- It is
- There are
- You find it
- You have
- You see, you hear, you feel
- You experience
- You gain
- You lose
- You eliminate [thing]

Behavior

- You do
- You act
- You [Name of Behavior]
- You find it easy to
- You find yourself
- You choose
- You see yourself
- You hear yourself
- You feel yourself
- You stop
- You avoid
- You change

Potential

- You can
- You are able
- You unlock
- You release
- You have the ability
- It's possible
- You learn
- You realize
- You increase
- You expand

Beliefs

- You believe
- You think
- You know
- You accept
- You're sure that
- You're positive that
- You trust
- You understand
- You have faith
- You decide
- You release the belief
- You reject

Notes

The Art of Suggestion: Targeting Layers, Continued

Values

- You feel
- It's important to you
- You're motivated to/by
- You desire
- You're driven to/by
- You're compelled to
- You're filled with
- You have the virtue
- [Name of value] becomes important
- It's unimportant
- It's irrelevant
- It's meaningless
- It's useless

Identity

- You are
- You become
- Your identity is
- Your character is
- Your integrity is

Notes

Step 8 – Bring Them Up

Now, it's time to bring them back to the wakeful state. Use the following script:

"In a moment I'm going to count from 1 to 5. With each number I count, you'll come 20% of the way back into the room – back to wakeful awareness, feeling wonderful and refreshed.

"One, beginning to notice a sensation in a hand or a foot."

"Two, noticing sounds in the room, perhaps sounds outside."

"Three, take a nice big deep breath in."

"Four, take a nice big stretch."

"Five, eyes open. Wide aware. Feeling wonderful and refreshed. Welcome back."

Notes

Review

1. Demystify Hypnosis (What hypnosis is not)

2. Explain Hypnosis (What hypnosis is)

3. Interview

4. Suggestibility Tests

5. Induction

6. Convincers

7. Change Work

8. Bring Them Up

Notes

Smoking Cessation

One Session of Smoking Cessation and One Follow Up

Three Major Concerns of Smokers:

You MUST address these before the therapy begins!

1. Addiction
2. Weight Gain
3. Nervousness

1. Addiction

I'm not here to say that cigarettes are or are not addictive, but I do want to have a conversation with you about your believing that you are addicted. And I'm wondering if you would be willing to keep an open mind about cigarettes. I always say that the mind is like a parachute – it only works when it's open, so would you be willing to have an open mind to some new possibilities about whether or not cigarettes are as addictive as they say? Great, so first let's define addiction. The type of addiction I want to talk about right now is the physical addiction, not the mental. We'll deal with the mental aspects of addiction in a moment. For now, let's just address the physical aspects of addiction.

Who tells us that cigarettes are addictive? (no matter what the response, lead them to the ultimate organization – the media) Has the media ever lied to you before? You see, the media is very certain that cigarettes are addictive, but I must share with you – thousands of people quit smoking each day, and not one of them experiences any kind of physical withdrawal symptoms that you would see in a normally addicting chemical like cocaine or heroin. I guess when I refer to addiction, what I'm talking about is the physical malfunction that bodies go through when being deprived of a substance upon which they have become dependent. No one's body malfunctions when they stop smoking cigarettes. In fact, think about it, how long can you go without a cigarette?

They will either answer with a short time frame or a very long time frame. If they respond with a short time frame (for example, 30 minutes) say the following...

Really? Do you sleep at night? How many hours (6 - 8 usually)? Do you smoke in your sleep? (no) Really, but can you go 6 - 8 hours during the day without smoking? (no) Why not? You do it at night don't you? People who are truly addicted to a chemical like heroin cannot sleep through the night, they have to get up to take a hit, just to go back to sleep. No one does that with cigarettes.

Notes

Some people will say that they do get up at night to smoke. Simply ask them if they get up to smoke, or if they get up to go to the bathroom, and while they are up, they smoke.

What about a movie? If you go to a really good movie, you can sit through the entire show without a cigarette, yet most people don't think they can go 2 hours without a cigarette, Doesn't this make you wonder how addictive cigarettes really are?

If they respond with a long time frame like 2 or 3 days, or even 2 or 3 weeks, say the following…

Exactly! Now how many crack addicts would say (their answer)? How many heroin addicts? For that matter, how many alcoholics? You see, even with just looking at your own life you have demonstrated that cigarettes do not have the same addictive characteristics biologically that truly addictive drugs do.

Now, I'm not into conspiracy theories or anything, but think about it, who benefits most by us thinking that cigarettes are addictive? The cigarette manufacturers! Wouldn't the best sales pitch in the world for any consumable product be, "If you start using these by age 12, you will smoke them for the rest of your life." It's got to make you think, doesn't it?

In fact, when I talk to people who become nonsmokers, the most severe physical problems I've ever had people tell me about is headaches – which were more than likely stress related anyway. I also hear about sore throats and shaking hands. I'll address the issue of shaking hands in a moment, but let's be honest about these so-called "symptoms." Are they not simply irritations instead? Irritation and malfunction are not the same things. They're not even in the same ballpark! Those symptoms do not cause malfunction. They just cause discomfort… which is not a word used to describe the addictive withdrawals from any other truly addictive drug.

So, is the biological aspect of addiction still a concern for you, or would you be willing to believe for the sake of this process that you are indeed not biologically addicted?

If they still insist that they are addicted, ask them what makes them so certain. Find out right now what their convincer is for being addicted. They either didn't listen to you, or you didn't talk about the one thing that makes them believe they are still addicted. No matter what their response, always ask them the question, "Yes, but did you malfunction?" The answer will always be no.

____

____

____

Notes

2. Weight Gain

Have you ever seen beef jerky at the super market? You know, that smoked meat that sits on the counter waiting to be bought? How much water do you think is in that meat? Right, not much at all. Well, what do you think you are doing to your body when you smoke it? It is a known fact that smoking causes dehydration. If you don't believe me, look at someone who has smoked for 50 or 60 years compared with someone who hasn't, their skin quality is completely different most of the time. When you become a nonsmoker, your body is going to naturally want to re-hydrate the cells that have dehydrated over the years. What this means is that you could gain anywhere from 2 - 5 pounds of cellular re-hydration. Now this is not fat, it is not water retention. It is simply the process of your body becoming denser – having each cell weigh slightly more because it is re-hydrated. Expect this. I would rather see you be 2 - 5 pounds heavier and a nonsmoker, than 2 - 5 pounds lighter and a smoker. Remember, this is water that your body needs anyway. Which would you rather be?

Some people worry that they are going to crave sweets when they become a nonsmoker. That's because, depending on what cigarette you smoke, each cigarette contains between 18 - 24% sugar! When tobacco is 'cured,' it is soaked in sugar water and then dehydrated. This is why some people's hands shake when they go without a cigarette for a while… it's called hypoglycemia, and shaking hands is one of the first symptoms of having low blood sugar. Now I can't tell you what to eat, but if I were going to find another source for sugar I would favor fruit. The natural sugars in fruit will counteract any cravings you may have for the lack of sugar from cigarettes. Would you be willing to accept a suggestion of increased fruit intake?

Finally, let me say this: In the highly unlikely event that you do gain more than 5 pounds, I will do a weight loss session for you for free. Now, is that fair? I will, however, ask you if you have been eating fruit or Twinkies and Ho-Ho's. If you say fruit, I will work with you, but if you've been using junk food to curb the sugar cravings… you are on your own, and I will not do a weight loss session for free, agreed?

Notes

3. Nervousness (AKA, Mental Addiction)

Here is what I can guarantee you. If you walk away here today as an EX-smoker, you will be nervous. If you walk away here today as an EX-smoker, you will be tense. If you walk away here today as an EX-smoker, you will be short tempered and mean. If you walk away here today as an EX-smoker, you will be craving cigarettes all of the time. How does that sound? (Bad) Well then might I suggest that you do not walk away here as an EX-smoker, but you will walk away here as a Nonsmoker. Think about the powerful identity shift that occurs with those three little letters. The difference between being an EX-smoker and a Nonsmoker is very subtle, yet very effective. I know that this may be difficult to understand, because you are looking at me through the eyes of a smoker, but in a moment, you are going to be looking at me through the eyes of a Nonsmoker. You see Nonsmokers don't worry about cigarettes, because they just simply don't want them. It's not a matter of should or shouldn't smoke, it's just a matter of not wanting to, because it's no longer your identity. Does this make sense?

Now, let's play a game, let's pretend that I am the world's most successful hypnotherapist. I have a 100% success ratio…I don't, but it's fun to pretend… everyone I work with becomes a nonsmoker with only one session. Do you think you will notice a void in your life? (wait for response)

You most assuredly will. Well, it's possible that you won't, but very few people become nonsmokers and completely forget about cigarettes, with no void what so ever. Those are the elite; however, the average person will experience a void.

The reason for saying that specific phrase is that nobody likes being known as average, so it places a covert desire deep within to be "one of the elite."

The funny thing is, when people experience the void in their life, they freak out and give false meaning to the void. They say, "Oh my God! I'm noticing a void. That must mean I want a cigarette." No, it just means you noticed the void. Don't give it any more meaning than it deserves. In fact, if you do experience a void THAT MEANS the hypnosis is working! Think about it: If the hypnosis weren't working, what would you automatically be doing? Right, smoking, but because the hypnosis is working, your unconscious mind now is not reaching for the cigarette and your conscious mind is catching up and wondering what it's supposed to do.

Another thing that people experience is an increased desire to play with their hands, or they become fidgety. What's funny is that they link up false meaning to the fidgeting. They say, "Oh my God! I want to do something with my hands. That must mean I want a cigarette." No, it simply means that you want something to do with your hands again. Don't give it any more meaning than it deserves. In fact, if you find yourself getting fidgety, THAT MEANS

Notes

the hypnosis is working! Think about it: You can probably get a cigarette out of the pack, lit, and in your mouth without even being consciously aware of it, can't you? Right, so when your unconscious mind no longer wants to smoke, and it stops doing it, you consciously catch up with it and wonder what you are supposed to do with your hands instead. You see, as human beings, we are very nervous creatures, and wanting something to do with your hands is not an exclusive trait to smokers. Nonsmokers like to do it too! So if you notice a void or want something to do with your hands, embrace those desires, but don't give them false meanings. Simply appreciate how well the hypnosis is working, and find something else to do, okay?

Notes

Weight Loss

Five Suggestions for Weight Loss

Behavioral changes for weight loss that work (10 lbs to 35 lbs easily)

1. Eat what you want
2. Eat only when hungry
3. Focus only on eating when eating
4. Put down food/utensils between each bite
5. Chew your food 30% more than usual (up to 32 times per bite)
6. Check your stomach between each bite and stop at a fullness six or seven on a scale of one to ten

Why not to do weight-loss hypnotherapy for deadlines or "events":

When people have a specific date by which they want to lose weight, their motivation to keep the weight off often goes away after the deadline has passed.

Ask them for permission before you recommend foods and exercise (Hypnotherapists are not licensed to recommend or prescribe):

"...Are there any foods you should/should not be eating? Would you like me to suggest to you that you increase/decrease your consumption of those foods?"

"...What kinds of exercise do you think you should/should not be doing? Would you like me to suggest to you that you increase/decrease those activities?"

Notes

Follow-Up Sessions

There are only three responses you'll hear from your clients when you call to follow-up. The paradigm below is for smoking cessation; however, it can be used for any standard behavioral therapy:

Answer #1 "I'm doing great!"

At this point, probe for problems, even if they haven't reported any. Ask questions like, "Have you had any temptations to _________ or have you been doing well? Have you noticed any 'voids' in your life where you don't know what to do? Give me some details. What, exactly, does 'I'm doing great' mean?"

If they do say that they have some voids, or temptations, but they've been handling them okay, then ask them, "Do you need any more sessions, or do you feel like you're doing okay on your own?"

If they say they want additional sessions, then they are probably not actually doing "great." Treat the call exactly as if they were to answer with the next possible answer.

Notes

Answer #2 "I'm doing okay," or "I'm doing terrible"

If they answered *okay*, there is probably no guilt for any "slip ups." However, there is still a need for a follow-up session. If the answer was *terrible*, then they are more than likely experiencing some sort of guilt, so that must be dealt with first. Usually, a casual "reframe" (from NLP) will work just fine. The following is an example of how you could provide your client with some perspective in order to help them feel good about their current situation. After all, feeling good will always serve them better than feeling bad. Guilt is a terrible motivator. This technique works for anything, but the example below is for smoking.

"Are you a meat eater or a vegetarian?"

If they answer *meat eater*...
You: "Have you ever just had a salad once for lunch without any meat ever?"
Client: "Of course."
You: "Why didn't you freak out and start calling yourself a vegetarian? Shouldn't you technically be a vegetarian and never eat meat again? Of course not! To call yourself a vegetarian after having only a salad just once is silly, and the same is true for thinking that you are still a smoker after you've smoked just a few cigarettes.

You know what you are? You're a nonsmoker who smoked a few cigarettes, just like there are meat eaters who occasionally eat just salad. Relax. Today you might be a nonsmoker that smokes three cigarettes, tomorrow you might be a nonsmoker who smokes one, the day after you might smoke four, after that two, but eventually, you'll just be a nonsmoker who doesn't smoke at all, because that's what you are, a nonsmoker."

If the answer was *vegetarian*…
You: "Have you ever eaten meat accidentally, or perhaps for the purpose of being polite at someone's home?"

They will always say *yes*. It is virtually impossible for a vegetarian to eat socially and not occasionally eat meat. It is possible that you may meet someone who is a hard-core vegan who grows their own food, but those people will not typically be your smoking cessation clients. For the vegetarians, say the same thing as above, but flip the argument to reflect their answer.

Notes

Two Reasons a Client May Continue to Smoke

1. Psychological

The void is too great and they want something to do with their hands. In this case, identify the places where they had difficulty, then provide them with a replacement behavior to do instead of smoking.

Link the new behavior up to the emotional need that they have for cigarettes. How to identify the emotional need is written in detail in the additional reference material.

2. Biological

They need the cigarettes for a biological benefit.

What possible benefits could smoking have? There is one ... Breathing! People who smoke take deep breaths of oxygen in between their puffs on the cigarette. Even though one out of five breaths are polluted with smoke, the other four are deep cleansing breaths.

Typically, people who are athletically fit have a much easier time quitting than those who are lethargic and lazy in their lives. Why? Athletic people have other channels for deep breathing, while people who live a more relaxed "couch potato" type life need cigarettes to get their standard deep breaths.

Notes

Answer #3 "No Change"

This rarely happens, but when it does, the following approach is very effective...

"Okay, let's imagine that there is a big screen TV here. And on the TV is you, living your life, smoking cigarettes, but wherever you go, you tell people that you are really committed to quitting smoking. But there you are, smoking in your car, smoking during breaks, smoking after meals, all the while, telling people you want to quit smoking." (At this point, change vocal tone into a hypnotic voice, and switch referential index for the person in the TV) "But the volume is broken on the TV, so we can't hear a thing that character is saying in the show. So you and I, we have to just look at the actions of that character, and make our decisions about who this person is based on the actions we see on the screen... So you tell me, based upon the actions of this character on the screen, is that character in the role of a nonsmoker or a smoker? Does that person really want to quit?" (Let them answer)

"So while I hear what you are telling me, your actions are sending a completely different message. Now that tells me that only one of two things are going on right now.

"Number one, you really don't want to quit, but you are here for someone else. Maybe your kids want you to quit, or your spouse wants you to quit, or maybe even your boss, but it's <u>other</u> people that want you to quit, not you. Now if that's what's going on here I want to tell you I admire that in you. It's incredibly noble for you to be here right now. Most people don't have the fortitude to even do this, so I admire you for that. And, as noble as that is, it's <u>not</u> enough of a reason to quit. You have to want to quit for you, not for anyone else.

"So if that's the case, I think we would be wasting our time to continue, so what I would like to do is give you half of your money back right now. We'll shake hands, and part as friends, and then in the future, when you finally decide to quit for <u>you</u>, you can come back and we'll do the process all over again for the second half of the payment.

"Now if you really <u>do</u> want to quit, then the second possibility may be occurring. You may actually want to quit, but sadly, I failed to communicate to you what this process is all about. Remember how I compared hypnosis to a book, and told you that the print on the page can't create emotions in your body, but it's how you interpret the print, just like how you interpret my words that make the changes? I'm sorry I didn't communicate that clearly.

"You see, hypnosis will never MAKE YOU a nonsmoker. Hypnosis will only MAKE THE PROCESS of quitting an easy one. But you have to be <u>so</u> willing to quit smoking that all I would have to do is say, (snap fingers) you are now a nonsmoker and you would be one.

"Are you so ready to quit that all I would have to do is say, (snap fingers) you are now a nonsmoker and you would be one? Because you have to be at that point in order for this to

Notes

work, so if you are, great, let's keep working. If not, then why don't I give you half your money back, and we'll part as friends."

Now at this point, they will probably take the money, but if they say they still want to do the hypnosis, sit them down and say, "(snap fingers) You are now a nonsmoker. Do the best you can, and I'll follow-up with you in one week."

They will usually be a little confused by this. But you must remind them that just *seconds* ago they said that they were so motivated that that's all you would have to do.

The reason for doing this is to determine the strength of their will power, for will power alone can get them to reduce their consumption at the very least. If they tap into the will power and really make an effort, they will likely be more successful in a follow-up session.

However, if they are smoking as much as ever that shows that they really do not want to quit.

Notes

Identifying Emotional Benefits

The following example is for smoking cessation; however, this paradigm can be used for any behavioral change that your client may be seeking.

“When you smoked that first cigarette after our session, I'm guessing that you came to some sort of an emotional crossroad – a point of decision if you will. Is that correct? I mean the cigarette didn't accidentally jump into your mouth, did it? You did decide, didn't you?

"Okay, so when you came to that crossroad, I'm guessing that you probably weighed your options. You knew you were going to feel awful about it later. You knew you were going to have to talk to me about it, too. But the temptation to smoke was so compelling that it overshadowed the negative consequences of smoking, right?

"So I'm curious, what was it that pushed you over the edge, and allowed you to smoke? What was it that you thought the cigarette would give you, regardless of whether or not it actually did? What was the emotion you were going for?”

Now at this point, your client will probably say "I don't know." This is the *make-it-or-break-it* part of the interview. Whatever you do, DO NOT SAY ANYTHING EXCEPT "I know you don't know, but if you did know, what would you say?" Sit back, be quiet, and let them talk it out. DO NOT OFFER SUGGESTIONS UNDER ANY CIRCUMSTANCES!!! It is important to realize that offering help to your client at this point will destroy the interview completely and literally ruin the effectiveness of the second session – even if you offer the smallest bit of advice.

Here's what will happen. Usually, they struggle, say they don't know a couple of times, and then start telling you a story about what happened. Pay no attention to the story. It will only distract you. Turn your ear toward one thing and one thing only – a positive, emotional word. Once you have that, you have the key. Here's an example of a typical response...

"I don't know, I just wanted the cigarette. There I was after dinner, and I was going crazy because I didn't know what to do with my hands, on top of that I was stressed out from my work that day, the boss barked at me and threatened to fire me if I didn’t hit my quota. Plus the dinner I was on was with a first date, and I was very nervous. So there I was, nervous, stressed out, and wanting something to do with my hands, because in the past, smoking after a meal made me feel confident that I could handle the situations of the day more effectively. So the cigarette would seem to take away all that stress, I guess."

Notes

Now on the surface, we might think that the client wanted to relax, but that actual word never came up. The only word that came up which was a positive emotional benefit was the word "confident". If you use any other word other than confident, you are putting words into their mouth, reading their minds (inaccurately), and not focusing on the real issue at hand. IF YOU USE ANY WORD OTHER THAN THE WORD THEY USE, THIS TECHNIQUE WILL NOT WORK!!!

Once you have the word, then you need to feed it back to them, but if you do it too quickly, you might come off as pompous or arrogant. Feed their answers back to them, but act as if the two of you are discovering something together. Here is an example of how the above hypothetical situation might have continued…

"Okay, let me make sure I'm hearing you correctly. What I'm hearing is that you were done with your meal, and you really wanted a cigarette, right? And at some level, you were hoping that the cigarette might make you feel more confident. I think that's the word you said, is that right? Okay, you wanted to feel more confident, and one of the ways in the past that you've accomplished that was by smoking a cigarette, right? Okay, so I guess what I'm hearing is that you really wanted to feel confident, but you didn't know any other way to achieve that other than by way of a cigarette? Is that right? Great so if you had some other way to feel confident, you wouldn't have needed the cigarette… because what you really wanted was to feel that confident feeling, not the cigarette, right?"

Now by doing it in this sort of self-discovering way, it gives the impression that you both are figuring this out together. It is possible, although unlikely, that your client may disagree with you at the end, and if this happens, just get to a higher level of emotional benefit. Simply say, "Oh, I'm sorry, then if you had the cigarette, and felt confident, what would that have done for you emotionally?" Now start back at the top, run through the process again until you get agreement.

Once you have the emotional need, during the follow-up hypnosis session, link that emotion up to a new behavior. If the new behavior includes something about deep breathing, then you will have conquered both of the needs that client may have for continuing to smoke.

Notes

Bonus: Self-Hypnosis

Which is Correct?

- ☐ I am relaxing
- ☐ You are relaxing
- ☐ He is relaxing or she is relaxing

Characteristics of Self-Hypnosis: ____

____

____

____

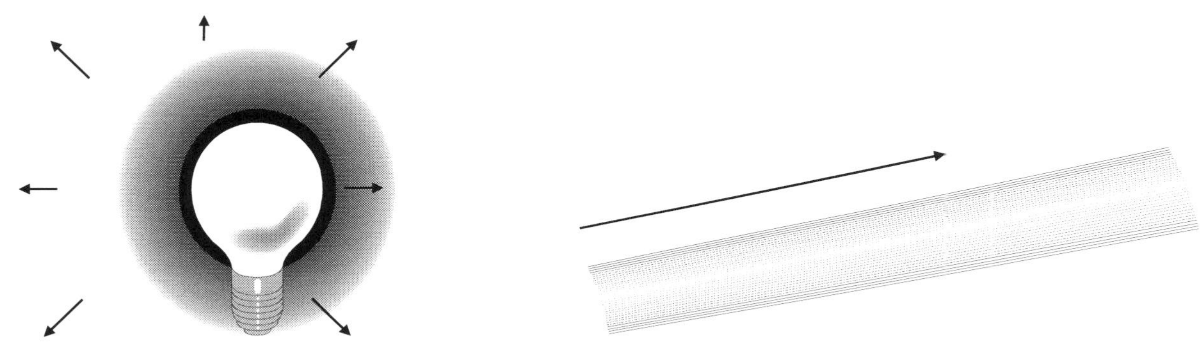

The most important aspect of self-hypnosis is ______________________

Steps for Self-Hypnosis

1. Rapid Induction
2. Convince Yourself
3. Offer Suggestions
4. Awaken

Notes

Scope of Practice

The specific applications of practice, or what a hypnotherapist may and may not do, is not defined in law in many places. The following is a list of common issues that hypnotherapists may be faced with on a daily basis. We have broken them into three areas. Category One is considered self-improvement, and you have the skills to deal with these issues based on this class. Category Two contains issues that are in a gray area and you may or may not need a referral and more skill. Category Three definitely needs a referral from a licensed practitioner prior to hypnosis. If you do choose to take any clients for medical or psychological diagnoses, you can use the client referral sheets in the bonus section on the website.

Category One Self-Improvement: OK!	**Category Two** Gray Area: Careful!	**Category Three** Referral Needed
Weight Loss	Self-Confidence	Diagnosed Mental Illness
Smoking Cessation	Procrastination	Diagnosed Physical Illness
Self-Improvement	Nail Biting	Extreme Nervousness
Relaxation Techniques	Exercise	Insomnia
Improve Memory	Assertiveness	Sexual Problems
Improve Concentration	Enthusiasm	Health Complaints
Improve Study Habits	Regression Work	Uncontrollable Anger
Exam Preparation		Extreme Guilt
Exam Anxiety		Depression
Improve Sports Ability		Pain Management
Speed Reading		Breast Enlargement
Enhance Creativity		Any True Phobia
Improve Salesmanship		PMS
Self-Hypnosis		Allergies
		Addictions

If you are a member of the International Board of Coaches and Practitioners, you may call the board with questions regarding scope of practice. Call in the US at: (888) 731-8375 toll-free, or from anywhere in the world, +1 (714) 243-8701 direct.

Notes

Sample Intake Form

Your Name/Company Name Here
Please complete this form (All information is strictly confidential)

Last Name (please print), First Name Middle Initial

Street Address City State Zip

( ) ( ) ( )
Work Telephone # Home Telephone # Mobile #

- - / /
Social Security Number Birth Date Email Address

M / F
Sex Marital Status Occupation

Have you ever been treated for an emotional problem? **Yes No**
If yes, please explain: ______________________________

Have you ever been treated for: (circle) **Diabetes - Epilepsy - Heart Disorder - Digestive Problems**

Have you ever been hypnotized before? **Yes No**
If yes, please explain: ______________________________

What do you want to accomplish through the use of hypnosis? ______________________________

Any previous efforts to solve this problem? **Yes No**
Results? ______________________________

How did you hear about us? (circle all that apply)

Medical Referral - Relative - Friend - Newspaper - Radio - Television - Phone Book
Other: ______________________________

Do you have any fears or phobias? ______________________________

I am willing to be guided through relaxation, visual imagery, creative visualization, hypnosis, and stress reduction processes and techniques for the purpose of vocational or avocational self-improvement. I understand that the hypnotherapy I am receiving is not a substitute for normal medical care and I have been advised to discuss this hypnotherapy with any doctor who is taking care of me now or in the future. Additionally, I should continue any present medical treatment and consult my regular medical doctor for treatment of any new or old illnesses.

Signature: ______________________ Date : ____________

Name I like to be called: ______________________

Notes

Marketing Don'ts and Do's

Don't

- Be average
- Serve "everybody"
- Advertise in newspapers
- Sit behind your computer all the time
- Expect a full schedule within 30 days

Do

- Be unique and remarkable
- Serve a specific niche(s)
- Create joint ventures
- Get out and speak publicly
- Be patient and persistent

Notes

Marketing Ideas

The following are some ideas to help you get started, and market yourself in an economic way. Please keep in mind, there are exceptions to every rule, and depending upon your demographic location, these tips will have greater effect in some places than in others.

1. Join your Chamber of Commerce:

When someone joins the Chamber of Commerce, it says, "I am employed, and I have disposable income, and I'm willing to invest it in things that will help me succeed." In addition to marketing yourself to gainfully employed people who will be able to hire you for hypnotherapy services, most members of Chambers of Commerce support heavily the idea of referrals and networking. Unfortunately, most people join Chambers thinking that once they join, the business will start to roll in. This is not true. You must take time to cultivate relationships inside the chamber. If you are a consistent presence in your chamber, it will eventually pay off.

2. Use Vista Print for marketing needs:

In the beginning of your business, there is no need to hire a printing company to customize brochures and business cards. Start with the generic brochures, business cards, letterhead, and envelopes designed by Vista Print. You can reach them at www.VistaPrint.com. Once you are producing a consistent income, then you may want to upgrade to a more professional media print or qualify for bulk rates. For now, Vista Print will work just fine.

3. Speak whenever you can, wherever you can:

Health clubs, yoga studios, hair salons, martial arts studios, book stores, Chambers of Commerce, schools, spiritual centers and churches – all of these places are usually very willing to have guest speakers. Create a 30-minute presentation that you can use to enlighten people on the benefits of hypnosis. When you are finished with your presentation, leave plenty of your brochures and business cards so they can contact you if they are interested. There are three sample presentation scripts in the bonus section on the website.

4. Use executive office suites for office space:

Most people believe that the first thing they need to do is rent a beautiful office in order to start their business. THIS IS THE LAST THING YOU SHOULD DO. First, start off with

Notes

executive office suites. These are offices that you can rent by the hour. They are fully furnished, and all you have to do is bring in your stereo and framed certification to place on the bookshelf, and you have a mobile office. No, they probably won't have recliners for your client to sit in, but they will have comfortable chairs that will work quite well. Once you are working enough to spend more money on executive office suites, then you know it is time to rent an office of your own. Another viable option is for you to find 5 locations strategically located within a specific geographic area and work one day each week out of each office. You can maximize your advertising dollar this way.

5. Set up a merchant account:

The public will perceive your company as being much more stable if you can accept Visa and MasterCard. Remember, everyone may not have $300 cash, but almost everyone has $300 on a credit card. You are much more apt to receive business if you can accept credit cards. PayPal, Square and Stripe have professional merchant services.

6. Get a toll-free number:

Even if you are only doing business locally, a toll-free number will convince your clients that you are serious about your business and can make you look more successful than even your largest competitor. Contrary to popular belief, toll-free numbers are not expensive if you go with the right provider. Try www.FreedomVoice.com. They have rates as low as $10 /mo for an introductory toll-free system with five voicemail boxes and the ability to forward calls to any phone on a time scale (so curious people don't wake you up at 3am!)

7. Write a book.

Nothing makes you more of an authority than writing a book. It's easier than you may think. Transform Destiny founder Michael Stevenson wrote his best-selling book, *Learn Hypnosis... Now!*, after attending this very course years ago. While the task may seem daunting, once you know the step-by-step formula, you can have your book done in no time. Visit www.PublishingToProfit.com to learn about his book writing/publishing course.

8. Send emails and postcards to past clientele five times each year.

Believe it or not, your clients will forget your name and lose your phone number. But if you remain in contact with them throughout the year, they will be able to send you referrals when people ask how they lost weight or stopped smoking.

Send both business correspondence as well as personal emails to keep your business top of mind. The service at www.SendOutCards.com is a great way to keep in touch automatically.

Notes

9. Get a Coach

One of the biggest mistakes most practice owners make is going it alone. Instead, find someone who has done it before you and created success. This allows you to not only know what to do to create success, but also what not to do, to avoid all the pitfalls and mistakes that usually come with achieving success.

We recommend joining the ***Accelerate NLP Training, Coaching and Mastermind Program*** from Transform Destiny. Not only will it give you the additional training you need to become an expert and help more people, but it will also give you the coaching you need to be successful in your practice, and the community you need to accelerate your growth. Ask your trainer or training manager about the *Accelerate NLP Program* while you are here at this training.

10. Don't Sell Your Time

One of the most common errors new practitioners make is selling sessions or hours of time. Your time is unappealing to your prospects. They don't want your time. What do they want? Results.

Successful hypnotherapy practitioners sell programs that promise results for their clients. Rather than just selling hours, sit down and ask yourself, "what does my client need to get the specific result they want?" Then create a program that includes those things. This will get you much further than someone who just sells hypnotherapy sessions.

Notes

Helpful Hints For Dynamic Brochures

A personal brochure is a prospecting tool designed to attract new clients to your practice. Its purpose is to establish a positive emotional bond between you and the reader before you ever meet. A well-designed and carefully written personal brochure conveys credibility and competence while at the same time making the reader feel comfortable in picking up the phone to call you. Unless it achieves those results, your brochure will be worthless, no matter how it looks or what it contains.

The personal brochure is your first opportunity to establish a strong foundation for future business relationships. It is *not* the place to impress potential clients with your products or to score resume points. Take full advantage of this opportunity, and make your personal brochure work hard for you.

Five Steps To Creating An Effective Personal Brochure

Step One: Pick a Single, Focused Benefit

You cannot be all things to all people. Select a specific benefit that is designed to attract your target market. The most effective personal brochures tell a story or give examples which showcase this benefit in an interesting way. Keep these questions in mind: "What single benefit is most important to my potential clients, and what can I share about myself which will drive this point home?"

Step Two: Write a Personal Biography

Regardless of what you are selling – financial services, widgets, consulting, or hypnosis – if you don't do a good job selling yourself, your products will remain on the shelf. By the time a potential client finishes reading your personal brochure, he or she should feel as if they really know you. Present the information as though you are sharing a part of yourself. Like a good Barbara Walters interview, you can establish this kind of rapport by revealing who you are as a human being, not as a salesperson. Include personal information which illustrates who you are and builds an emotional connection between you and the reader.

Your personal biography should account from half to three-quarters of the brochure's entire contents. Resist the temptation to talk about your therapeutic services for at least the first two paragraphs. Even though you are selling yourself, don't frame it as a hard sales pitch. If the reader feels that you are pushing yourself on them, they will be less likely to do business with you.

Notes

If your practice is affiliated with a company, limit company and service information to one or two paragraphs. Present your company as a support system and capitalize on the power of your company name. The link between your image and your established company name increases your credibility in the minds of potential consumers.

Step Three: Follow These General Writing Guidelines

Use the third person, objective point of view in writing the text. Third person gives the impression that you are reporting facts, not engaging in self-important bragging. Keep the text positive. Do not mention pitfalls, dangers or other scenarios which may frighten the reader. For example, "Hypnosis cannot make you do things against your will."

Present your material in paragraphs. As much as salespeople don't believe it, long story-formatted text outsells short text every time. Use bullets sparingly as they can break up the natural flow of an idea.

Step Four: Create a Knockout Cover and an Appealing Layout

The central design element of your personal brochure is the front cover. The most compelling personal biography, or the most creative and effective presentation of your business philosophy is meaningless unless your prospects actually pick up the brochure in the first place. The cover must stimulate a reader's curiosity, announcing loudly and unmistakably, "Pick Me Up!" Do not place any images or text on the cover that refer directly to your company, products or services. Large format covers attract more attention, so use a large formatted image that is easily recognized by your target market.

Your personal brochure should be inviting to the eye, making the reader want to start and finish it. Include lots of open (or white) space. Don't clutter the design by cramming it with long, dense blocks of text or too many photographs or graphics. In addition to a generous use of white space, photographs and graphics will give your brochure a look of professionalism. As important as the content is, the look and feel of your brochure convey more about your image than words ever will. A well-designed brochure builds instant credibility in the reader's mind.

Unusual sized brochures dramatically increase readership rates. The best shape for brochures is usually a square, because it is often perceived as an invitation. The most effective brochure sizes, when folded, are 6"x 6", 7"x 7", or 8"x 8".

Notes

Personal Brochure Uses

The purpose of your personal brochure is to attract new clients. Be lavish in distributing them. Don't hoard them. They can't do the job they were designed to do if they sit in a box under your desk or on shelves in the back room. We have found that the clients who get the best results from their personal brochures are those who print in quantities of at least 2,500 and usually 5,000 or 10,000. With a generous print run, you won't worry about running out and you will feel comfortable and eager to distribute them.

So, where should you use your personal brochure? In any and every situation where you would normally use your business card.

Networking	Advertising
Telemarketing	Presentations
Lead Follow-up	Current Clients
Potential Clients	Public Speaking

Guidelines for Writing Your Personal Biography

People do business with people they feel comfortable with. Sharing your personal story gives you a chance to introduce prospective clients, not to an intimidating hypnotherapist, as sometimes seen in the movies, but to a real, caring person, someone with similar concerns and interests, and someone who makes them feel, "They're just like me!"

One approach you can use to develop your personal story is the "self-interview." You can conduct this interview yourself, or ask a friend or family member to do it. Record the information either into a tape recorder or by writing it down. Record your answers and use them as the basis when your write your personal brochure.

1. What has been your greatest accomplishment in life so far?
2. Describe the most difficult challenge you have ever faced. How did you meet it? What did you learn from it?
3. Describe an important lesson you learned from someone in your family. Who taught you the lesson? How has that lesson influenced you?
4. What single life-experience has created the person you are today?
5. If you had to limit your life to one point in time, what would you say was the defining moment? What about this moment made it so significant?

Notes

Additional Reference Materials

Notes

The Psychology of Suggestions

What is a suggestion?

1. A suggestion is any single thought, series of thoughts, ideas, words, beliefs, or actions given in any manner – direct, indirect, conscious, unconscious, that changes or alters a person's normal behavior pattern.

2. A suggestion is any process whereby a person accepts a command, a plea, a proposition, a thought, idea, belief, or any direction to be acted upon in the absence of any critical or reflective thoughts which would normally occur.

3. A suggestion is any process whereby one person or group may have subtle or direct influence on another's behavior in any state whether it be the conscious, unconscious, or hypnotic state.

Suggestions come in a variety of ways. They influence us every day of our lives and have done so since the day of our birth. Below are a few examples of the types of suggestions that may have had a bearing on changing or altering our normal behavior patterns.

Direct Suggestions are any verbal statement or physical action that is direct, to the point and without camouflage. Direct suggestions are given in an "authoritarian" or "persuasive" manner.

- Everybody stand up. (authoritarian)
- Everybody, please stand up. (persuasive)
- Pass the sugar.
- Come here.
- Eat your food.

Indirect/Inferred Suggestions are generally not recognized as suggestions. This is because they are primarily non-verbal, often only motions or sounds, and the subject is not even aware of their influence.

Notes

Indirect:

- Cough ... and you cause others to cough.
- Yawn … and you cause others to yawn.
- Smile … and you cause others to smile.
- Look up at tall buildings… and you cause others to look up.

Inferred:

- Pointing a finger at someone, suggesting they come here
- Pointing a finger at someone, suggesting they leave the room
- Nodding your head to indicate your approval or disapproval
- Making a fist at someone, suggesting violent action

Prestige Suggestions are those you accept and act upon as your very own without "second thought" or contradiction because they were given by a person of prestige whom you like, trust, respect or in whom have some confidence. Prestige suggestions may enhance your life in some way – socially, economically, politically, academically, emotionally, intellectually, physically or psychologically.

Examples of people who have prestige:

- Doctor
- Lawyer
- Teacher
- Clergy
- Politician
- Hypnotist
- Speakers
- Friends
- Parents
- Authors
- Entertainers
- Athletes

Non-Prestige Suggestions are personalized conditioned reflex suggestions that influence a person's conduct in the waking state.

- Music suggests happiness, sadness, dancing, singing, romance, etc.
- Sight or smell of food suggests hunger, or possibly nausea.
- Rain suggests freshness, cleanliness, depression, coziness, etc.
- Street noises suggest hyperactivity or excitement.

Notes

Environmental Suggestions are those that affect your 5 human senses, VAKOG (Visual, Auditory, Kinesthetic, Olfactory, Gustatory)

- Clear sunny days with bright blue skies and comfortable temperatures make us feel happy, content and full of vitality.
- Dismal gray days of rain, snow, or fog make us feel "down in the dumps" or sluggish.
- Extreme heat or cold can generate feelings of discomfort or pain.
- Well-decorated or well-ventilated working or living conditions can cause us to react with a feeling of well-being and elation.

Conditioned Reflex Suggestions cause a person to form a habit pattern or way of life based on a continuous, constant, repetitious learning process. This learning process is reflex conditioning, and it can be a conscious or a subconscious process that will influence or alter a person's behavior pattern with or without his/her awareness. Conditioned reflex suggestions affect all five of the human senses and they can be self-induced or externally induced.

- Good Humor man rings his bells, you automatically buy his ice cream
- Parades, mob violence, political rallies, all may stimulate your physical/emotional responses
- Religious ceremonies accept dogmas and doctrines without question
- Vulgarity or obscenities stimulate positive or negative emotions or physical responses

Emotional Suggestions are those that raise your emotional or sensory state thereby setting into motion any feelings, sensations or emotional responses.

- Shouting/making verbal threats can cause a state of fear or panic
- Antagonizing can cause anger
- Gentleness/empathy can cause happiness, laughter or crying

Unconscious Suggestions are those comments, statements, suggestions or stimuli received by a person while in some form of altered, receptive state which an outside source absent-mindedly or indiscreetly induces. Generally, neither part is consciously aware of the consequences.

Notes

Social Suggestions are those suggestions designed to lead or appeal to an individual for the purpose of conformity. Experiments in social suggestions show that people tend to "follow the crowd." Individuals "give in" to peer pressure.

- Politics – people tend to vote for the person who appears to be "the peoples' choice"
- In the world of fashion – people "follow the trends." To be in style is to be accepted. It is a way of belonging and being "in" with the crowd by inference.

Autosuggestion is the process of giving suggestions to one's self, either in the "waking state" or any "alpha or meditative state".

Hetero-Suggestions are those given by one person to another in any manner.

Post-Hypnotic Suggestions are those suggestions that are specifically designed to be implanted during the hypnotic state, then used or acted upon after the person has been "hypnotically awakened."

Pre-Hypnotic Suggestions are those generally used with "deep" hypnotic subjects to "pre-talk" their suggestions in a conscious state prior to hypnosis induction. The "pre-talk" will include the goal or purpose of the induction about to take place, plus the time frame, or the conditions for awakening from the hypnotic state.

Negative Suggestions are designed to tell the client not to manifest something, be it a behavior, emotion or thought.

- Don't feel stressed.
- Don't get angry.
- You will not smoke.
- Don't roll your eyes at me.

While generally not recommended to use in hypnosis, negative suggestions can sometimes produce a desirable effect:

- Don't go into a trance too quickly.
- Don't think about relaxing too deeply.
- Don't smile as you think about your future.
- Don't enjoy this process too much.

Notes

Words that may indicate negative suggestions are being used:

Try	Maybe	Hope
Never	Don't	Can't

Positive Suggestions are designed to create images of the desired outcome.

- Do feel happy.
- You can relax deeply.
- You will succeed.

Words that may indicate positive suggestions are being used:

Succeed	Will	Know
Always	Do	Can

Notes

Post-Hypnotic Suggestions

Creating suggestions that operate at a later time

A post-hypnotic suggestion is a suggestion that activates and operates at a time after the induction of trance. The time of the activation of the suggestion can be minutes later or months later.

1. Usually Requires Medium-to-Deep Trance:
While not all clients can do these right away, a post-hypnotic suggestion generally requires a trance which is at a medium-to-deep level. One key element is a state of amnesia for the suggestion.

2. Make the Suggestion Direct and to the Point:
While suggestions should, at first, be given in an indirect way, post-hypnotic suggestions should be direct and to the point. This is true for any suggestions given while the client is in deep trance.

3. Tell the client what the Trigger for the Post-Hypnotic Suggestion will be:
Tell the client what will set off the activation of the post-hypnotic suggestion. For example: "When I pull my ear, you will fall deeply into a hypnotic state, totally relaxed, and completely at ease."

4. Tell the Client what to do:
Be specific about what you tell the client you want them to do. For example: "... you will automatically drink a glass of water..."

5. Tell the Client when to do it:
This tells the client when to do the post-hypnotic suggestion. For example: ".... and you will do it any time you may have thought of a cigarette."

6. Embed the Suggestions:
Make sure that you lead into the suggestions in the opposite way that you lead out of the suggestions. For example:

Metaphor part I → End Result Imagery part I → Post-Hypnotic Suggestions → End Result Imagery part II → Metaphor part II

7. Test:
Test the suggestion to make sure that it produces the expected results.

8. If appropriate, remove the suggestion:
Any post-hypnotic suggestions created for experimental purposes must be removed at the end of the session. For example: "... come fully awake. Good. Any and all hypnotic suggestions relating to hypnotic phenomena are hereby removed." If the post-hypnotic suggestions are created for positive behavioral shifts, then, of course, they would still stay in effect. For example: "...Every time you walk through the threshold of your office doors, you will feel an incredible feeling of decisiveness take over as you begin to plan your day."

Notes

Waking Suggestions for Moderate Pain Control

Note: It is illegal to do pain control for medical conditions and diagnoses without a written referral from a medical doctor.

Direct Suggestion - If your client is highly suggestible, you can simply tell them that their hand is becoming numb, and often it will. I do this by first telling them that their opposite hand is becoming very sensitive to touch... so sensitive, in fact, that the slightest touch will feel painful and they will want to move their hand or hide it from me. I will usually accomplish this by putting a small drop of water on their hand telling them it is a chemical called sensodine 7 – a standard chemical used by doctors to irritate the skin for tests. [I have no idea if such a chemical exists, I'm actually just putting water on their hand, but it sounds great and creates a wonderful reaction for the suggestible people] Once it is dry, I test the hand by touching it. If they do not feel pain, then the reduction of pain is not available through direct suggestion, and I have spared them from a painful pinch. If it does work, then I can assume that if they can increase pain through imagination, they can also decrease pain through imagination. I will then place another drop of water on their opposite hand and rub it in. Telling them that this is a topical anesthesia used by most dentists to numb the surrounding area they will work on. Once it is dry, I test it by pinching, and if they created the pain on the other hand, they also remove the pain on this hand. No pun intended, but they go hand in hand with one another!

Dissociation – This technique requires the client to imagine they are either floating out of their painful body, or that the affected body part is floating away from the actual body. Another version is to ask the painful sensation to float out of the body and travel to the part of the universe that would be more suitable for the pain. Either way, the idea is to float one aspect of themselves far enough away that they lose access to the pain. This is a good short-term fix, but I do not recommend they leave the office this way, because they can sometimes feel disoriented. This technique works best if taught as a "Band-Aid" technique to use whenever the pain flares up.

Recalling Past Experience – This works off of the principle that if you recall a time in your past when you felt an intense sensation, you will begin to feel that sensation again. For example, if you remembered a time when you were happy, you would begin to feel happy. If you remembered a time when you felt sad, you would begin to feel sad. The same is true for feeling numb. If you remember a time when you were anesthetized, that part of your body may begin to feel anesthetized. It is important to ask the client in advance for a non-traumatic time in their past that they can remember being anesthetized. Since most anesthesia is associated with at least some trauma, it is unlikely that you will find many clients who can have a pleasurable anesthesia memory. A rare exception is the occasional person who has had a pleasurable dental experience.

Notes

Jamming Dialogue – If you preoccupy the client's internal dialogue with discussion about anything other than pain, they will not be able to feel pain. I usually get them to begin saying out loud the phrase "totally numb, totally numb," over and over again as though they are talking in their sleep. Before I begin to pinch, I tell them to focus on the sounds of the vowels in the phrase "totally numb, totally numb," and then I pinch the back of their hand. Later, I talk to them about the practice of using specific words in their life. If they say they have "pain," they feel it. This is where I tell them that pain control is about shifting certain things in their life, starting first with the words they use to describe the sensation in their affected body part. If I can get them to change the words they use on a daily basis to describe the pain, the pain will begin to subside. For example, instead of consistently complaining about their "injured back," allow them the opportunity to still speak of their back, but suggest that they refer to it instead as a "healing back." This small linguistic shift can make monumental changes in their experience.

Location Elimination – This technique can be performed in the waking state, and it is the fastest way I know to remove pain. I prefer to use it exclusively for headaches; however, it will also work on any other body part as well. It generally takes between 1 ½ to 2 minutes to completely remove the pain. I ask them to answer questions without pointing to the location of their painful body part. Then I begin to ask them questions that cut the location of the headache in half by height, width, and depth. For example, "... is your headache to the left or the right of your head? *Right* Is it to the front or the back? *Front* The top or the bottom? *Top* The right of the right or the left of the right? *The left of the right* Above the eye or below the eye? *Above*" I continue this process until the location of the headache is so small that their mind gets frustrated and admits that it doesn't even have any pain. Below is a visual description of what will be going on in their head. The gray color represents the location of the pain.

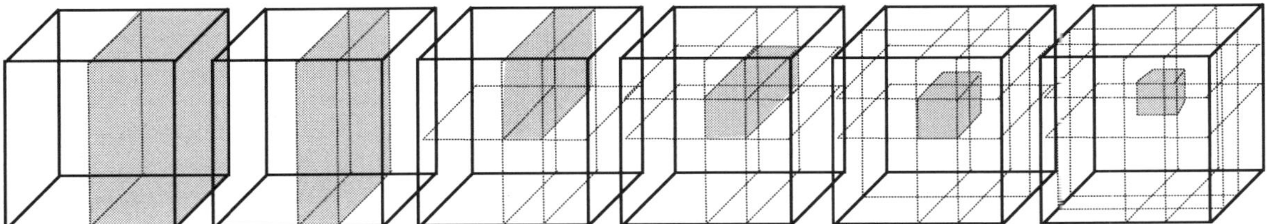

Notes

Glossary

ABREACTION - The release of emotionally charged material from the mental process.

ACADEMIE DE SCIENCES- A French scientific organization.

AGE PROGRESSION - Advancing the subject's age level while in the hypnotic state.

A. M. A. - The American Medical Association.

AMNESIA- The loss of memory. The amnesia, which frequently occurs in hypnosis, may be either spontaneous or induced by suggestion.

ANESTHESIA- Insensibility to feelings of pain.

ANALIZATION - To study the factors of a situation in detail in order to determine a solution or outcome.

ANIMAL MAGNETISM - Mesmerism; the principles advocated by Frederich Anton Mesmer.

ANIMATION, SUSPENDED- Temporary suspension of the vital functions.

ANIMOSITY - Resentment tending toward hostile action.

ANXIETY- Painful uneasiness of mind.

AUTO-CONDITIONING - A series of experiments designed for bringing one's subconscious under control.

AUTOHYPNOSIS- Self-hypnosis; automatic hypnosis.

AUTOMATIC CONTROL- The controlling of one's mental process automatically.

AUTONOMIC NERVOUS SYSTEM - A part of the peripheral nervous system regulating involuntary responses especially those concerned with nutritive, vascular and reproductive activities.

AUTOSUGGESTION - Self-suggestion, as distinguished from suggestions coming from another.

BAQUET - French word for tub; a device used by Mesmer for inductions.

BLIND SPOT- An area in one's discernment where one fails to exercise understanding.

BRAIDISM - Those theories advocated by James Braid.

BRITISH ASSOCIATION - British medical group.

CATALEPTIC - A muscular seizure.

CATALEPTIC RIGIDITY - Muscle rigidity; number ten (10) on the Davis-Husband scale.

CATALEPTIC TRANCE - The second stage of hypnotic state; medium trance state.

CAUSATIVE FACTORS - The conditions leading to the development of mental and physical disorders.

CLAIRVOYANCE - The ability claimed by some individuals to discern objects not actually present.

CONDITIONED REFLEX - A reflex that responds automatically.

CONDITIONED SUBJECT- A person who has been initiated to hypnotic induction.

CONDITIONING - A series of inductions making certain ideas or things acceptable to the subject's subconscious mind.

CONSCIOUS - State of being aware of an inward state or an outside fact.

CONSCIOUS AUTOSUGGESTION - The persistence in consciousness of impressions gained through subconscious training.

CONSCIOUS DISTORTION - Responses to the senses lessened in degree by interference during consciousness.

CONSCIOUS LEVEL CONTROL- The principles of autosuggestion in the waking state.

CONSCIOUS RECALL- Memory.

CONVULSION - An involuntary general paroxysm of muscular concentration.

COUEISM - The principles of autosuggestion as advocated by Emile Coue.

Notes

COUNTER REGRESSION - The process of returning from a regressed state to a normal state; this is a normal part of the process of waking from hypnosis.

COUNTER SUGGESTION - A suggestion that is made to counter the effect of suggestions, which have been given to induce hypnosis.

DAVIS-HUSBAND SCALE - Chart of determining hypnotic state depths.

DEFENSE MECHANISM - A mode of behavior, or a belief, adopted by the subject, often unconsciously, to conceal the true state of matters pertaining to himself.

DISSOCIATION - The segregation from consciousness of certain components of mental processes, which then function independently.

DRUG HYPNOSIS (NARCOHYPNOSIS) - Sleep induced by narcotics (sodium amatol and sodium pentothal) aided by hypnotic suggestions.

DYNAMIC METHOD - Method of using the subject's distortions for inducing the hypnotic state.

DIANETICS - Science founded by mathematician Hubbard, utilizing, but not admitting to, all the principles of hypnotism.

EFFECT- Created condition with hypnotic suggestions.

E. C. T. - (ELECTRIC CONVULSIVE THERAPY) - Electric shock treatment.

ELECTROENCEPHALOGRAPH - An apparatus for detecting and recording brain waves.

EMOTIONAL OUTLET- A habit pattern formed to release emotional tension.

EXCITORY PERSONALITY- One who stimulates or irritates an organ or tissue.

E. S. P. (EXTRA SENSORY PERCEPTION) - Perception that is not mediated by the sense organs.

EXTROVERT- One who interests himself with the outside world rather than himself.

FAITH HEALER- One who practices treatment of diseases by religious belief and prayer.

FASCINATION POINT- The object upon which the subject fixes his gaze in hypnotic method

FATHER HYPNOSIS - The use of a forceful tone for inducing hypnotic state.

FLACCIDITY- A looseness; an absence of tone seen in muscles of persons relaxed in hypnosis.

FLUIDISM - Mesmer's theory of a life-sustaining fluid contained within each body.

FRACTIONATION - The procedure of hypnotizing the subject, waking him and re-hypnotizing him a number of times in the same session; an effective means of increasing hypnotic depth.

FREE ASSOCIATION - Spontaneous unrestricted associations of loosely linked ideas or mental images having very little rational sequence or continuity.

GLOVE ANESTHESIA- A loss of sensation in an area corresponding to that covered by a glove.

HALLUCINATIONS- A perception arising in the absence of appropriate external stimuli.

HEMOPHILIAC - One who is affected by hereditary disease occurring only in males but transmitted genetically by females, characterized by excessive bleeding.

HETEROSUGGESTION - Suggestions made by operator and directed to subject.

HYPNOANALYSIS- Hypnosis utilizing psychoanalytic techniques.

HYPNODISC- A disc with spirals used in inducing hypnotic state.

HYPNODONTICS- The science of dental hypnosis.

HYPNOGRAPHY- A technique in hypno-analysis in which the hypnotized subject is brought to express psychological conflicts in painting.

HYPNOID- A state resembling sleep.

HYPNOS- Greek word for sleep.

Notes

HYPNOSIS - Name given to the hypnotic state by Dr. James Braid; a repressed state of mental functioning in which ideas are accepted by suggestion rather than logical evaluation.

HYPNOTHERAPY- Treatment by hypnosis.

HYPNOTIC INSURANCE - A predetermined code by the operator transposed to his subject to return him to the hypnotic state instantly.

HYPNOTIC PASSES- Those gestures or movements made by the hypnotist over the body of the subject without actually touching them.

HYPNOTISM - The science of hypnosis.

HYPNOTIST- The operator.

HYPNOTIZE - The act of inducing the hypnotic state.

HYSTERIA- Emotional excitability due to mental causes.

HYPERESTHESIA- A high degree of sensitivity.

IDEO-MOTOR ACTIVITY- Non-voluntary movement produced as the direct expression of an idea.

INSTATE SLEEP SUGGESTION - A method of inducing sleep automatically in post-hypnotic control.

KINESTHETIC DELUSIONS- Total anesthesia.

LAY HYPNOTIST- The term applied to persons outside the medical profession who utilize hypnotic techniques in their practice.

LETHARGIC SLEEP- Light hypnotic state, characterized by little or no post-hypnotic control; first hypnotic state.

LETHARGY- A condition of drowsiness or stupor.

MAGNETIC FLUID- See fluidism.

MAGNETISM - The belief, founded by Mesmer, in which the magnetic power of one human being could control another person.

MAGNETIZER - One who uses the first principles advocated by Mesmer.

MANIA- Excessive enthusiasm; a craze.

MASS HYPNOSIS- Induction of a group of people simultaneously.

MECHANICAL DEVICE - An object, such as a hypno-disc, used to induce the hypnotic state.

MEDIUM - A person supposed to be susceptible to supernormal agencies and able to impart knowledge derived from them or to perform actions impossible without their aid.

MESMERISM- Those hypnotic principles advocated by Mesmer.

MESMERIST- One who employs the principles of Mesmerism.

METRONOME- An instrument used for marking exact time.

MINERAL MAGNETISM - The belief that magnets could control effects in the body.

MODERATE EFFECT GROUP- Simple experiment that can be performed after reaching the relaxation stage of hypnosis, such as temperature changes.

MONOIDEISM - A term employed by Braid for waking-hypnosis and the lighter stages of the hypnotic state.

MOTHER HYPNOSIS- Soft, lulling tones used to induce hypnosis.

MOTIVATION - The force that determines patterns of behavior.

MOTOR ACTIVITY- Designating or pertaining to a nerve or nerve fiber, which passes from the central nervous system or a ganglion to a muscle and by the impulse which it, transmits or causes movement.

NARCOHYPNOSIS- See Drug Hypnosis.

NERVOUS SLEEP- The hypnotic state wherein conscious is inactive while subconscious is alert and suggestible.

NORMAL SLEEP- The state wherein the conscious sleeps normally.

Notes

OBJECTIVITY- Ability to view events, ideas and phenomena as external and apart from self-consciousness, detached and impersonal.

OCCULT- The unseen, beyond the bounds of ordinary knowledge.

OPERATOR- Hypnotist.

PAIN - Distressing feeling.

PANACEA- A cure-all.

PHENOMENON - An exceptional, unusual, or abnormal thing or occurrence.

PHOBIA- Morbid fear.

PHRENOLOGY- The study of the conformation of the skull as indicative of mental faculties.

PLANTS- Conditioned subjects believed to be used in stage hypnotism.

POSTHYPNOTIC SUGGESTION - Those suggestions made during the hypnotic state to be carried out after awakening.

POST TRANCE CONDITION - Enrapport state in which the subject maintains a certain degree of susceptibility consciously.

PRECAUTIONARY SUGGESTION - See Hypnotic Insurance.

PRECONDITIONING - The psychological impression you make on your subject concerning hypnosis.

PREHYPNOTIC SUGGESTION - A visual or verbal suggestion used to indicate hypnotic conditions.

PREHYPNOTIC TESTS- Tests based on reflexes accompanied by suggestion to create certain effects.

PRESTIGE SUGGESTIONS - Suggestions that are willingly accepted based upon the operator's level of prestige.

PROFESSIONAL HYPNOTIST- One who makes a living employing the principles of hypnotism.

PROJECTION - The attributing of one's own feelings to someone else.

PSYCHOANALYSIS- A method of evaluating persistent subconscious ideas.

PSYCHOLOGICAL CRUTCH - Leaning heavily on another person to create certain effects.

PSYCHOLOGIST- One who investigates the phenomena of consciousness and behavior.

PSYCHOSOMATIC- Functional inter-relationship between mind and body.

RAPPORT- Relation of harmony, comfort, accord; state of being in tune with your subject.

RATIONALIZATION - To evaluate with adequate analysis.

REALITY- True state of anything.

REFLEXIVE TESTS- See Pre-hypnotic Tests.

REINCARNATION - The belief of a successful return to life.

RIGIDITY - Muscular tenseness.

SCHOOL OF NANCY - Those ideas sponsored by A. A. Liébeault and H. Bernheim; the establishment of scientific hypnosis so called for its geographic location in Nancy, France.

SELF-CONTROL- Conscious autosuggestion.

SELF-HYPNOSIS- Placing one's self into a hypnotic state.

SELF RAPPORT- Being in tune with one's self.

SHOCK TREATMENT- A doubtful method of therapy;electric current to induce an artificial state of shock.

SKEPTIC - One who doubts or disbelieves.

SLEEP INDUCTION - Inducing the hypnotic state.

SLEEP RECORDINGS- Records and tapes prepared for use in inducing a hypnotic state.

SODIUM PHENOBARBITAL- A drug used in narco-hypnosis.

Notes

SOMNAMBULISTIC STATE - A state of deep relaxation; third and final hypnotic state; usually the hypnotist's objective with his subjects.

STAGE HYPNOTISM- Entertaining hypnotism.

SUBCONSCIOUS- The nature of mental operation not yet present in consciousness.

SUBCONSCIOUS CONTROL- Automatic suggestion.

SUBJECT- One who is experimented with or tested.

SUGGESTION - An idea that is offered to the subject for uncritical acceptance.

SUGGESTIVE THERAPY- The removal of symptoms by hypnotic suggestion.

SUSCEPTIBILITY- Capability of receiving impressions; sensibility.

SUSPENDED ANIMATION - See Animation, Suspended.

SYMPTOM REMOVAL- Removal of pain that denotes a condition.

THERAPEUTIC - Of or pertaining to the healing arts; curative.

TIME DISTORTION - Unexplainable lapse of time during the hypnotic state by the subject.

TRANCE - A state of profound abstraction.

TRANCE CONDITION - The state of being hypnotized.

TRANCE DEPTH - The level of relaxation achieved by the subject.

TRANCE DURATION - Time spent in the hypnotic state.

TRANCE MEDIUM - The use of a hypnotized subject to foresee the future.

TRANSFERENCE - The self-made science of Professor J. M. Charcot.

TRAUMA - Injury; shock or the resulting condition.

TWILIGHT SLEEP- The state between consciousness and natural sleep.

UNCONDITIONED SUBJECT- A person who has never been approached with the hypnotic process.

VASOMOTOR - Physical activity over which the subject has no control.

WAKING HYPNOSIS- Hypnotic suggestions accepted by the subject in the waking state.

WILL- A thought conveyed by the subconscious that becomes reality.

WILL, CONSCIOUS- Imaginary mental force.

WORD ASSOCIATION - Mental reaction to word stimuli.

Notes

Training Contacts & Networks

Keep in touch with us and with those who you meet and connect with at the training. Make note of all your contacts' information here:

Name	Phone	Email	Notes
Transform Destiny	800-497-6614	cs@transformdestiny..com	Success experts

Notes

Notes

Notes